WHY DO WE GO TO CHURCH?

PASTOR DR. CLAUDINE BENJAMIN

WHY DO WE GO TO CHURCH? Copyright @ 2025. Pastor Dr. Claudine Benjamin. All rights reserved.

For more information or to book an event, contact:
inspiredtowinsouls@gmail.com

Published by:

Editor: Cleveland O. McLeish (Author C. Orville McLeish)

ISBN: 978-1-965635-67-4 (paperback)

DEDICATION

This book is lovingly dedicated, first and foremost, to the Lord Jesus Christ, the Head of the church, who gave His life for our redemption. Without His grace, there would be no reason, no message, and no power in these pages.

I also dedicate this work to the body of Christ worldwide—to pastors who labor faithfully, to leaders who serve tirelessly, and to every believer who gathers week after week, not out of duty but out of love for God. May this book renew your passion and remind you of the eternal value of the church.

Finally, I dedicate it to those who may have grown weary, discouraged, or distant from the fellowship of believers. This book is my prayer for you: that you will return, be restored, and rediscover the joy of belonging to God's house.

ACKNOWLEDGMENT

I give honor and glory to God, who placed this burden in my spirit and gave me the strength to carry it through to completion. Truly, all wisdom and revelation come from Him.

To my family, who have always encouraged my walk with the Lord and supported the calling on my life—thank you for your prayers, patience, and love.

To the spiritual mentors and pastors who have guided me, I owe a debt of gratitude. Your example of faithfulness to the church has been a living testimony that inspired these words.

To my church family, who have taught me through both joys and challenges what it truly means to walk together in love and fellowship—you are living proof of God's design for His people.

And finally, to every reader who picks up this book—you are the reason this work exists. My prayer is that you will not only understand why we go to church, but also experience the fullness of God's presence each time you gather with His people.

AUTHOR BIO

Pastor Claudine Benjamin is a devoted servant of Christ, a passionate preacher of the gospel, and an author committed to equipping the body of Christ to walk in truth, purpose, and spiritual maturity. With a heart for souls and a burden for the church, Pastor Claudine has dedicated her ministry to teaching believers the importance of staying rooted in God's Word and faithful to His call.

Her writings reflect a deep love for scripture, a prophetic urgency for revival, and a pastoral desire to see God's people flourish. She believes the church is not just a building but the living body of Christ, designed to bring hope, healing, and transformation to a broken world.

Through preaching, teaching, and writing, Pastor Claudine continues to challenge and encourage believers to remain steadfast in their faith, pursue the presence of God, and embrace the mission of the great commission. Her books are an extension of her ministry, carrying the same fire, compassion, and biblical depth that mark her life's work.

When she is not preaching or writing, Pastor Claudine is deeply engaged in prayer, discipleship, and mentoring—raising up a new generation to stand boldly for Christ.

TABLE OF CONTENTS

Part I

The Biblical Foundation

Part II

Why We Go to Church Today

Part III

Misunderstandings and Challenges

Part IV

The Blessing of Belonging

Part V

The Call to Commitment

INTRODUCTION

REDISCOVERING THE PURPOSE OF GATHERING

Why do we go to church? For some, it is simply a family tradition passed down through generations. For others, it is a matter of convenience, a place to meet friends, or an obligation to "check off" once a week. Still, for many believers, it is a holy and treasured rhythm of life—an opportunity to gather in God's house, worship His name, and be strengthened by His Word and His people.

This book seeks to answer the question not from opinion, culture, or convenience, but from the unchanging truth of God's Word. At a time when church attendance has declined in many places and the value of the local church is often questioned, it is vital to return to the biblical foundation for why we gather. The church is not a man-made invention. It is not a club, an organization, or a social gathering. The church is the body of Christ (**see 1 Corinthians 12:27**), the bride of Christ (**see Ephesians 5:25–27**), and the pillar and foundation of the truth (**see 1 Timothy 3:15**). To neglect the church is to neglect what Christ Himself loves, purchased with His own blood, and entrusted with His mission.

TRADITION, ROUTINE, OR TRUE DEVOTION?

Across the ages, the church has been central to the lives of God's people. Yet, in today's culture, a pressing question emerges: *Why do we go to church?* Is it out of tradition, because it's what our parents or grandparents always did? Is it simply routine, a Sunday morning activity slotted between breakfast and the rest of our day? Or is it out of true devotion—a heart overflowing with love for God, eager to worship, grow, and serve?

The way we answer this question will determine whether the church remains a living movement of God's Spirit or merely a ritualistic gathering without power. Jesus Himself warned that outward observance without inward devotion leads to hypocrisy: **"These people honor me with their lips, but their hearts are far from me. They worship me in vain; their teachings are merely human rules." (Matthew 15:8–9 - NIV).**

CHURCH AS TRADITION

Tradition in itself is not evil. Paul encouraged believers to **"stand firm and hold fast to the teachings we passed on to you" (2 Thessalonians 2:15 - NIV).** Biblical tradition, when rooted in truth, safeguards the faith and connects us to the testimony of those who came before us.

However, when churchgoing becomes only tradition, stripped of living faith, it can trap us in empty formality. Israel fell into this error, maintaining sacrifices, festivals, and rituals while their hearts drifted from God. The prophet Isaiah declared: **"Stop bringing meaningless offerings! Your incense is detestable to me." (Isaiah 1:13 - NIV).**

Today, many attend church out of family heritage or cultural expectation. Sunday worship becomes part of identity, but not transformation. The danger? Tradition without encounter leads to a shell of religion without the Spirit of life.

CHURCH AS ROUTINE

For others, going to church is a matter of routine. It's penciled into the weekly schedule—like brushing teeth or going to work. The rhythm is predictable, and though routine can be stabilizing, it often lacks passion.

Jesus confronted the church at Ephesus for falling into such complacency: **"You have forsaken the love you had at first." (Revelation 2:4 - NIV).** They had good works, order, and discipline, but the flame of first love was flickering.

Routine Christianity produces believers who show up but rarely grow up. They sit in pews, sing songs, and hear sermons, yet their hearts are unchanged. Like Israel in the wilderness, they circle the mountain repeatedly but never enter the Promised Land (**see Deuteronomy 2:3**).

The danger of routine is that it inoculates us with just enough religion to keep us from true revival.

CHURCH AS TRUE DEVOTION

True devotion is the heartbeat of authentic worship. It is not driven by family tradition or weekly routine, but by love for God. The psalmist cried, **"I rejoiced with those who said to me, 'Let us go to the house of the Lord'" (Psalm 122:1 - NIV).**

Devotion transforms the church from a place we go to into a fellowship we belong to. It shifts focus from attendance to encounter, from ritual to relationship, from spectating to serving.

In **Acts 2:42**, the early believers **"devoted themselves to the apostles' teaching and to fellowship, to the breaking of bread and to prayer." (NIV).** Their devotion birthed revival, unity, and power. This is the model of the church Christ established—not a tradition to maintain nor a routine to check off, but a community on fire with devotion to the living God.

- The Pharisees kept traditions and routines but missed the Messiah standing in front of them (**see John 5:39–40**).

- Mary of Bethany broke her alabaster jar in true devotion, while others criticized her for not following routine (**see Mark 14:3–9**).

MODERN CHURCH LIFE

Some show up because it's what "good Christians do." Others attend mechanically but leave unchanged. Yet a remnant longs to gather out of hunger for God's presence. Which group do we belong to?

A CALL TO EXAMINE OUR HEARTS

We must ask ourselves: *Am I attending church out of cultural expectation, weekly habit, or heartfelt devotion?*

- If tradition is your only reason, ask God to breathe life into it.
- If routine drives you, ask God to set your soul ablaze again.
- If devotion is your motive, keep pressing deeper into His presence.

Jesus told the Samaritan woman, **"a time is coming and has now come when the true worshipers will worship the Father in the Spirit and in truth, for they are the kind of worshipers the Father seeks." (John 4:23 - NIV).**

God is not seeking churches full of spectators but worshippers aflame with Spirit-filled devotion.

A GOD-ORDAINED GATHERING

The very word "church" comes from the Greek *ekklesia*, meaning "the called-out ones." The church is not a building of bricks and mortar, but a people called out of darkness into His marvelous light **(see 1 Peter 2:9)**. When we gather on Sundays or at midweek services, we participate in something supernatural. We align ourselves with the early believers in **Acts 2:42**, who **"devoted themselves to the apostles' teaching and to fellowship, to the breaking of bread and to prayer." (NIV).**

God designed the church as the place where His presence is manifested, His Word is proclaimed, and His people are transformed. It is here that the broken find healing, the weak find strength, and the discouraged find hope. In a world full of distractions, the church remains a sacred space where heaven and earth intersect, and believers are reminded of their eternal purpose.

MORE THAN A PERSONAL FAITH

In modern culture, faith is often portrayed as a private, individual matter—"just me and God." While personal devotion is essential, the Bible never presents Christianity as a solitary journey. From Genesis to Revelation, God works through a community. Adam was given Eve, Abraham was promised descendants, Israel was called as a nation, and the New Testament church was birthed as a fellowship of believers.

We cannot fulfill the "one another" commands of scripture—love one another, bear one another's burdens, encourage one another, pray for one another—in isolation. Church is where these commands come to life. Without gathering, we risk reducing Christianity to a self-centered spirituality, detached from the mission of Christ and the needs of others.

THE MISSION OF THE CHURCH

At its core, the church is not only a place of gathering but a launching ground for mission. Jesus declared, **"Therefore go and make disciples of all nations…" (Matthew 28:19 - NIV).** That commission was not given to individuals in isolation, but to His disciples as the foundation of His church. When we gather, we are equipped to scatter—to go into our homes, workplaces, schools, and communities carrying the light of Christ. The church is both the training ground for believers and the sending ground for missionaries, witnesses, and soul-winners.

To abandon the church is to weaken the mission. To embrace the church is to align with God's heartbeat for the world.

A CALL TO RECOMMITMENT

This book is not written to condemn but to awaken. It is a call to rediscover the joy, privilege, and necessity of gathering with God's people. For those who have been wounded by church experiences, may you find healing in these pages. For those who have grown weary in well-doing, may you find renewed strength. For those who have drifted away, may you hear the Spirit's gentle invitation: **"Return to My house, return to My people, return to My presence."**

As you journey through the chapters, you will see that attending church is not about obligation, but about opportunity—the opportunity to meet with God, grow in faith, build relationships, receive instruction, and walk in obedience to His Word. It is an opportunity to be part of something bigger than yourself: the glorious, victorious church that Jesus Christ is building, against which the gates of hell shall not prevail (**see Matthew 16:18**).

Let us embark on this journey together with open hearts and minds, asking the Lord to renew our vision of His church. For the question is not merely, *"Why do we go to church?"* but rather, *"What happens to us and through us when we do?"*

READER'S CHALLENGE: PREPARING YOUR HEART

Before you move forward in this book, I want to challenge you to pause and reflect. The purpose of this journey is not just to read words on a page but to allow the Holy Spirit to renew your vision of the church and your place in it.

Take a moment and ask yourself:

- What has been my personal reason for going to church?

- Have I seen church primarily as an obligation, a tradition, or a place of convenience?

- What would it look like if I went to church with the expectation of encountering God's presence, growing in His Word, and serving His people?

- How might my life, family, and community change if I became fully committed to the body of Christ?

A PRAYER FOR RENEWAL

"Lord, open my eyes to see Your church the way You see it. Remove any bitterness, distraction, or complacency that keeps me from fully committing to the fellowship of believers. Rekindle in me a passion for gathering with Your people, hearing Your Word, and serving in Your house. Let me not be a casual attender but a faithful disciple, planted and fruitful in Your kingdom. In Jesus' name. Amen."

A STEP OF ACTION

As you begin this book, make a personal commitment: "I will approach church, not as something optional, but as a vital part of my spiritual walk. I will go expecting to meet with God and to give as much as I receive."

DECLARATION

"I will not go to the house of the Lord out of empty tradition or lifeless routine. I will go with true devotion, hungry for His presence, ready to serve, worship, and be transformed. My church attendance will be an overflow of my love for Christ, not a substitute for it."

PART I

THE BIBLICAL FOUNDATION

CHAPTER ONE

GOD'S DESIGN FOR THE CHURCH

I magine, for a moment, a grand architect drawing up plans for a magnificent building. Every detail is considered, every measurement precise, every material chosen with care. Now imagine ignoring those blueprints and constructing the building according to personal ideas or convenience. The result would be unstable, unsafe, and eventually, it would collapse.

This is exactly what happens when we try to redefine the church outside of God's design. Many today view church as optional, outdated, or man-made. Yet the scriptures remind us: *the church is not a human invention—it is God's blueprint, ordained before the foundation of the world, purchased by the blood of His Son, and sustained by the Holy Spirit.*

CHRIST, THE BUILDER OF THE CHURCH

The foundation of the church rests upon Christ Himself. In **Matthew 16:18**, Jesus declared to Peter: **"I will build my church, and the gates of Hades will not overcome it." (NIV).**

Notice three things:

1. **Jesus is the Builder** — not man, not tradition, not denominational structure.

2. **The church belongs to Him** — His church, not ours.
3. **The church is victorious** — hell itself cannot overpower it.

When we gather for church, we are not attending a man-made institution. We are stepping into the living, breathing body that Christ is actively building in the earth.

THE CHURCH IN GOD'S ETERNAL PLAN

The church was not an afterthought. From Genesis to Revelation, God always intended to have a people set apart for His glory.

- In the Old Testament, Israel was called to gather as a covenant people around the tabernacle and temple (**see Exodus 25:8**).

- In the New Testament, believers gathered regularly "in one accord" (**see Acts 2:46**).

- Ultimately, in eternity, the redeemed will gather as a great multitude from every nation to worship before the throne (**see Revelation 7:9–10**).

The church is a reflection of heaven on earth—a foretaste of the eternal assembly to come.

THE CHURCH AS THE BODY OF CHRIST

Paul describes the church as Christ's body:

"Now you are the body of Christ, and each one of you is a part of it." (1 Corinthians 12:27 - NIV).

This means the church is not a loose collection of individuals but an interconnected organism. Just as a body cannot function with disconnected members, neither can believers thrive apart from the church.

- Christ is the Head (**see Colossians 1:18**).
- Believers are members with different roles and gifts (**see Romans 12:4–5**).
- The Spirit unites us into one body (**see 1 Corinthians 12:13**).

To reject the church is to reject Christ's body. To neglect gathering is to cut ourselves off from the very source of nourishment and purpose.

THE CHURCH AS THE BRIDE OF CHRIST

Not only is the church His body, it is also His bride. Ephesians 5:25–27 reminds us:

> **"Christ loved the church and gave himself up for her to make her holy... to present her to himself as a radiant church, without stain or wrinkle or any other blemish, but holy and blameless." (NIV).**

The intimacy of this image should transform how we view the church. If Christ loved the church enough to die for her, how can we treat her as optional? If He is preparing her in holiness for eternity, how can we distance ourselves from her fellowship?

THE CHURCH AS THE DWELLING PLACE OF GOD

The church is also the dwelling place of God's presence. Paul wrote:

"In Him the whole building is joined together and rises to become a holy temple in the Lord. And in Him you too are being built together to become a dwelling in which God lives by His Spirit." (Ephesians 2:21–22 - NIV).

Every time we gather, the Spirit of God is uniquely present in the corporate assembly (**see Matthew 18:20**). This does not negate personal devotion, but it affirms that there is a dimension of God's presence reserved only for the gathered body.

PRACTICAL APPLICATION

If the church is Christ's body, His bride, and His dwelling, then attending church is not just a weekly ritual—it is an alignment with God's eternal design.

- **We are built stronger together.** Like living stones, we are "being built into a spiritual house" (**see 1 Peter 2:5**).

- **We are safer together.** Sheep without a fold are vulnerable to wolves (**see John 10:12**).

- **We are more fruitful together.** The Spirit gives gifts "for the common good" (**see 1 Corinthians 12:7**).

When we forsake gathering, we weaken our growth, our protection, and our mission. But when we embrace God's design, we flourish in His house (**see Psalm 92:13**).

or. The true church is not shrinking—
she is being refined, prepared as a radiant bride for the coming
King.

REFLECTION CHALLENGE

1. Do you view church as God's divine design or as a human
   institution?

2. How does recognizing the church as Christ's body and bride
   change your attitude toward attending?

3. Are you planted and flourishing in God's house, or are you
   trying to survive spiritually in isolation?

PRAYER OF RENEWAL

"Lord Jesus, thank You for building Your church. Thank You that
I am a part of Your body, Your bride, and Your dwelling place.
Forgive me for any complacency, excuses, or wounds that have
caused me to distance myself from Your design. Plant me firmly in
Your house and help me to see the church the way You see her—
chosen, loved, and radiant. Strengthen me to be faithful, committed,
and fruitful in Your body. In Jesus' name. Amen."

STEP OF ACTION

This week, take time to read **Acts 2:42–47**. Write down three things the early church devoted themselves to. Then pray over how you can intentionally live out those same commitments in your church community.

CHAPTER TWO

THE PURPOSE OF GATHERING

When coal is removed from a fire and left to the side, it quickly grows cold. But when placed back among the other coals, it regains its flame and burns brightly again. In the same way, a believer separated from the fellowship of the church soon grows spiritually cold. But when we gather together, our faith is stirred, our fire is rekindled, and our hearts are strengthened.

Gathering with the church is not just a suggestion; it is a command and a necessity for the believer's spiritual health. The question is not merely *"Why go to church?"* but *"What happens when we gather?"*

THE COMMAND TO GATHER

Hebrews 10:24–25 gives us clear instructions:

> **"And let us consider how we may spur one another on toward love and good deeds, not giving up meeting together, as some are in the habit of doing, but encouraging one another—and all the more as you see the Day approaching." (NIV).**

This passage highlights three truths about gathering:

1. **It stirs us up** — Gathering provokes us to love and good works.
2. **It exhorts us** — We are encouraged by one another's faith.
3. **It prepares us** — As Christ's return draws near, the church must be united and strong.

To forsake the assembly is to weaken ourselves and to disregard God's clear command.

THE POWER OF CORPORATE WORSHIP

Psalm 95:1–2 calls us to:

> **"Come, let us sing for joy to the Lord; let us shout aloud to the Rock of our salvation. Let us come before him with thanksgiving and extol him with music and song." (NIV).**

Worship can be private, but it reaches its fullness when it is corporate. In **Acts 16:25–26**, Paul and Silas prayed and sang hymns together in prison, and the power of God shook the foundations of their cell. There is a dimension of breakthrough reserved for believers who lift their voices together in unity.

Jesus Himself promised:

> **"For where two or three are gathered together in My name, I am there in the midst of them." (Matthew 18:20 - NIV).**

This is not about numbers; it is about presence. God dwells in the praises of His people (**see Psalm 22:3**), and when His people gather, His glory is revealed.

THE MINISTRY OF THE WORD

When the church gathers, the Word of God is proclaimed with power. **Romans 10:17** declares:

> **"Consequently, faith comes from hearing the message, and the message is heard through the word about Christ." (NIV).**

The preaching of the Word is not a lecture or motivational speech. It is the Spirit-empowered declaration of truth that brings conviction, encouragement, and transformation. In Acts 20:7, the early church gathered on the first day of the week to break bread and to hear Paul preach. Teaching was central to their gatherings.

Gathering ensures that we are fed spiritually, corrected where needed, and equipped for the work of ministry (**see 2 Timothy 3:16–17**).

FELLOWSHIP AND MUTUAL ENCOURAGEMENT

The word fellowship (koinonia) means more than casual friendship. It is a deep spiritual sharing of life. In **Acts 2:42**, the early believers devoted themselves to "the apostles' teaching and to fellowship, to the breaking of bread and to prayer."

Gathering reminds us that we are not alone. We are part of a family. Ecclesiastes 4:9–10 teaches:

> **"Two are better than one, because they have a good return for their labor: If either of them falls down, one can help the other up. But pity anyone who falls and has no one to help them up." (NIV).**

When we gather, we strengthen the weak, comfort the hurting, and rejoice with those who rejoice. Church is the place where "iron sharpens iron" (**see Proverbs 27:17**).

THE CHURCH AS A SPIRITUAL REFUGE

In a world filled with hostility toward faith, the church is a place of refuge and strength. David declared in **Psalm 27:4**:

> **"One thing I ask from the Lord, this only do I seek: that I may dwell in the house of the Lord all the days of my life, to gaze on the beauty of the Lord and to seek Him in His temple." (NIV).**

For David, the house of God was not a burden but a delight. It was the place of safety, beauty, and intimacy with the Lord. Likewise, our gatherings today should be places where weary souls find rest, broken hearts find healing, and sinners find salvation.

PRACTICAL APPLICATION

Gathering with the church is not about habit—it is about health. A Christian without fellowship is like a soldier without an army, a sheep without a flock, or a coal removed from the fire.

- When we gather, we are encouraged in faith.
- When we gather, we are strengthened for service.
- When we gather, we are prepared for Christ's return.

To miss these gatherings is to miss opportunities for growth, protection, and transformation.

PROPHETIC INSIGHT

We live in an age where many are drifting from the church. Some claim, *"I don't need church to be a Christian."* Others are content with online sermons or occasional attendance. But the Spirit of God is sounding an alarm: the closer we come to the return of Christ, the more we must gather.

The enemy's strategy is isolation. A disconnected believer is a vulnerable believer. But God's strategy is gathering. A united church is an unstoppable church.

REFLECTION CHALLENGE

1. Do you see gathering with the church as optional or essential?

2. Have you allowed busyness, convenience, or personal offense to keep you from consistent fellowship?

3. How can you shift your perspective to see church as a place of encounter, encouragement, and equipping?

PRAYER OF RENEWAL

"Heavenly Father, thank You for the gift of gathering with Your people. Forgive me for the times I have neglected or taken lightly the assembly of believers. Rekindle in me a love for corporate worship, a hunger for the preaching of Your Word, and a commitment to fellowship. Plant me deeply in Your house and surround me with brothers and sisters who will strengthen my faith. Help me to be a source of encouragement to others as we prepare for the return of Christ. In Jesus' name. Amen."

STEP OF ACTION

This week, commit to attending at least one church service with full intention. Go not only to receive but also to give encouragement. Greet someone new, pray with someone who needs strength, or share a word of hope. Watch how God moves when you engage fully in the purpose of gathering.

CHAPTER THREE

JESUS AND THE EARLY CHURCH EXAMPLE

E very successful movement has a pattern, a model that inspires its followers. Athletes study film of past champions. Musicians learn from the masters who came before them. In the same way, the church today must look back at its original pattern—Jesus Christ and the early believers—if we are to remain true to our calling.

Too often, the modern church measures itself by numbers, programs, or popularity. But God never intended His church to be built on human strategies. The early church, birthed in the power of the Spirit, provides the blueprint for what the church is meant to be: simple, Spirit-led, and steadfast in mission.

JESUS AS THE MODEL FOR GATHERING

Before the church was born at Pentecost, Jesus Himself modeled the importance of gathering. **Luke 4:16** tells us:

> **"He went to Nazareth, where he had been brought up, and on the Sabbath day he went into the synagogue, as was his custom. He stood up to read." (NIV).**

Even the Son of God made it His custom to gather in worship. He did not neglect the assembly but honored it. In **Matthew 18:20**, He promised His unique presence among those who gather:

"For where two or three gather in my name, there am I with them." (NIV).

If Jesus valued gathering, how much more should we?

THE BIRTH OF THE CHURCH AT PENTECOST

The church was born in a prayer meeting. **Acts 2:1–2** declares:

"When the day of Pentecost came, they were all together in one place. Suddenly a sound like the blowing of a violent wind came from heaven and filled the whole house where they were sitting." (NIV).

The Spirit did not fall on isolated individuals scattered across the city, but on believers united **"with one accord in one place."** Unity and gathering invited the outpouring of the Spirit.

From this, we learn:

1. The church is birthed in prayer.
2. The church is sustained in unity.
3. The church is empowered in fellowship.

THE DEVOTION OF THE EARLY CHURCH

Acts 2:42–47 gives us one of the clearest pictures of church life:

"They devoted themselves to the apostles' teaching and to fellowship, to the breaking of bread and to prayer. Everyone was filled with awe at the many wonders and signs performed by the apostles. All the believers were together and had everything in common... They broke

bread in their homes and ate together with glad and sincere hearts, praising God and enjoying the favor of all the people. And the Lord added to their number daily those who were being saved." (NIV).

Notice the four pillars of their devotion:

1. **The Apostles' Teaching**—They gathered around the Word of God.
2. **Fellowship**—They shared life deeply with one another.
3. **Breaking of Bread**—They worshiped together and remembered Christ's sacrifice.
4. **Prayer**—They sought God's presence as a united body.

The result was power, unity, generosity, and growth.

SIGNS, WONDERS, AND GROWTH

The early church was marked not only by devotion but by demonstration. **Acts 5:12** tells us:

"The apostles performed many signs and wonders among the people. And all the believers used to meet together in Solomon's Colonnade." (NIV).

Where there was unity and gathering, there was also power. The Lord Himself confirmed their gatherings with miracles, healings, and deliverance. Their meetings were not lifeless rituals but supernatural encounters.

As a result, **"the Lord added to their number daily those who were being saved." (Acts 2:47 - NIV).** The church grew not by marketing or entertainment, but by the power of the Spirit working through a devoted people.

PRACTICAL APPLICATION

The early church gives us a pattern that is still relevant today:

- **Teaching**—Gather to be grounded in truth.
- **Fellowship**—Gather to encourage and support one another.
- **Worship**—Gather to exalt Christ and remember His sacrifice.
- **Prayer**—Gather to seek God's presence and power.

When these elements are present, the church is healthy. When they are neglected, the church drifts from its calling.

PROPHETIC INSIGHT

Today's church is often tempted to trade simplicity for sophistication. We add programs but lose prayer. We pursue crowds but neglect discipleship. We build buildings but forget fellowship.

But the Spirit is calling us back to **Acts 2**—to purity, to devotion, to power. The church that will withstand persecution and impact the nations is not the church of entertainment, but the church of Pentecost.

REFLECTION CHALLENGE

1. Are you devoted to the same things the early church was devoted to?

2. How can you model the simplicity and power of the **Acts 2** church in your life and in your congregation?

3. Do you go to church merely to attend, or to participate in prayer, fellowship, and worship?

PRAYER OF RENEWAL

"Lord, thank You for the example of Jesus and the early church. Forgive me for any way I have settled for a shallow or casual approach to church. Stir in me the same devotion that marked the believers of **Acts 2**. Let my life be rooted in Your Word, strengthened in fellowship, enriched in worship, and empowered in prayer. Make me a part of a church that reflects Your Spirit's power and draws others to salvation. In Jesus' name. Amen."

STEP OF ACTION

This week, choose one element of the early church's devotion (teaching, fellowship, breaking bread, prayer) and commit to practicing it intentionally. For example, consider joining a Bible study, inviting a fellow believer over for a meal, or attending a prayer meeting. Watch how God deepens your faith when you follow the pattern of the early church.

PART II

WHY WE GO TO CHURCH TODAY

CHAPTER FOUR

TO ENCOUNTER GOD'S PRESENCE

A traveler once entered a grand cathedral in Europe. Though he had visited many historical sites before, something was different here. As the choir sang and the congregation prayed, he was overcome with a sense of awe—not because of the architecture, but because of the undeniable presence of God. Tears flowed as he whispered, *"Surely, the Lord is in this place."*

Church is not about the building, the music, or the programs—it is about the presence of God. When we gather as His people, we enter into the divine privilege of meeting with the Creator of heaven and earth.

GOD'S PROMISE OF HIS PRESENCE

From the beginning, God's desire was to dwell with His people. In **Exodus 25:8**, God commanded Moses:

> **"Then have them make a sanctuary for me, and I will dwell among them."**

This desire continues throughout scripture:

- God's glory filled the tabernacle (**see Exodus 40:34–35**).
- His presence filled Solomon's temple so powerfully that the priests could not stand to minister (**see 2 Chronicles 5:13–14**).

- Jesus, "Immanuel—God with us," walked among men (**see Matthew 1:23**).
- Today, His Spirit dwells in His church, both individually and corporately (**see 1 Corinthians 3:16**).

When we gather, we do not gather for a program; we gather to encounter His presence.

JESUS' PROMISE IN THE GATHERING

Jesus affirmed the unique presence of God in the assembly:

> **"For where two or three gather in My name, there am I with them." (Matthew 18:20 - NIV).**

While God is everywhere, His manifest presence is revealed in a special way when His people come together in unity. This is why **Psalm 22:3** declares:

> **"Yet you are enthroned as the Holy One; you are the one Israel praises." (NIV).**

When the church worships, God dwells in the midst of His people. His presence brings healing, deliverance, and transformation.

THE POWER OF HIS PRESENCE IN WORSHIP

Worship is not about style, tempo, or talent. It is about creating a dwelling place for God's glory. Jesus told the Samaritan woman in **John 4:23–24**:

> **"Yet a time is coming and has now come when the true worshipers will worship the Father in the Spirit and in**

truth, for they are the kind of worshipers the Father seeks. God is spirit, and his worshipers must worship in the Spirit and in truth." (NIV).

This means worship is not confined to location but flows from sincerity and truth. Yet when believers unite their worship, the atmosphere shifts. In **Acts 16:25–26**, Paul and Silas sang hymns together in prison, and the very foundations of the jail shook. Their worship brought freedom—not only for themselves, but for everyone around them.

THE TRANSFORMING PRESENCE OF GOD

Moses knew that without God's presence, gathering meant nothing. He prayed in **Exodus 33:15**:

"If Your Presence does not go with us, do not bring us up from here." (NIV).

Church without the presence of God is nothing more than a social club. But when His presence fills the house:

- The sinner is convicted (**see John 16:8**).
- The sick are healed (**see James 5:14–15**).
- The weary find rest (**see Matthew 11:28**).
- The believer is strengthened (**see Isaiah 40:31**).

Every true revival in history has been marked by one thing: a fresh, overwhelming sense of God's presence in the midst of His people.

PRACTICAL APPLICATION

When you go to church, do not go merely to "attend." Go to encounter God. Prepare your heart before service. Enter His gates with thanksgiving and His courts with praise (**see Psalm 100:4**). Expect Him to speak through His Word, to move in worship, and to touch lives at the altar.

When we shift our perspective from routine to encounter, every gathering becomes a moment of transformation.

PROPHETIC INSIGHT

Today, many churches risk becoming performance-driven, with lights, sound, and programs but little true presence. But God is raising up a generation of worshipers who long not for entertainment but for encounter.

The Spirit of the Lord is restoring the fear of God in His house. People will once again walk into church and cry, **"Surely the Lord is in this place." (Genesis 28:16 - NIV).** The church that carries His presence will be the church that shakes the nations.

REFLECTION CHALLENGE

1. Do you see church as a place of routine or as a place of divine encounter?

2. How do you prepare your heart before going to church so that you can experience God's presence?

3. Are you hungry for His presence, or satisfied with programs and traditions?

PRAYER OF RENEWAL

"Lord, I desire more than anything to encounter Your presence. Forgive me for the times I have gone to church casually, without expectation or preparation. Awaken in me a hunger for Your Spirit and a reverence for Your house. Let my worship create a dwelling place for Your glory. May my church be filled with Your presence so that lives are healed, souls are saved, and Your name is exalted. In Jesus' name. Amen."

STEP OF ACTION

This week, prepare for church differently. Spend time in prayer before the service, asking God to reveal Himself. Enter with expectation, worship wholeheartedly, and watch how His presence moves among His people.

CHAPTER FIVE

TO HEAR AND OBEY GOD'S WORD

A farmer may have the richest soil and the best seeds, but without planting and watering, there will be no harvest. In the same way, a believer may have good intentions, but without the Word of God being sown into their heart, there can be no lasting fruit.

This is why the church gathers—not only to worship, but also to hear and obey the Word of God. Without the Word, worship is incomplete. Without the Word, fellowship is shallow. Without the Word, service has no direction. God's Word is the foundation upon which the church stands.

THE CENTRALITY OF THE WORD IN THE CHURCH

From the very beginning, the church has been built upon the teaching of God's Word. **Acts 2:42** tells us:

> **"They devoted themselves to the apostles' teaching and to fellowship, to the breaking of bread and to prayer." (NIV).**

Notice the first thing mentioned—teaching. The Word was central to the life of the early believers. It was not an afterthought or a side activity; it was the anchor of their faith.

Paul commanded Timothy:

"Preach the word; be prepared in season and out of season; correct, rebuke and encourage—with great patience and careful instruction." (2 Timothy 4:2 - NIV).

Hearing the Word is not optional for a believer; it is essential.

THE WORD BRINGS FAITH

Romans 10:17 reminds us:

"Consequently, faith comes from hearing the message, and the message is heard through the word about Christ." (NIV).

Faith does not come by opinion, tradition, or feelings. Faith is born and strengthened by the living Word of God. Each time we gather, God uses His Word to ignite faith in our hearts—faith to be saved, faith to be healed, faith to be sent.

THE WORD BRINGS CONVICTION AND CORRECTION

Hebrews 4:12 declares:

"For the word of God is alive and active. Sharper than any double-edged sword, it penetrates even to dividing soul and spirit, joints and marrow; it judges the thoughts and attitudes of the heart." (NIV).

When the Word is preached, it confronts sin, pierces the conscience, and calls us back to holiness. A church that does not preach the Word will produce believers who live in compromise. But when the Word is faithfully proclaimed, lives are transformed and aligned with God's will.

THE WORD EQUIPS US FOR SERVICE

Paul wrote:

> **"All Scripture is God-breathed and is useful for teaching, rebuking, correcting and training in righteousness, so that the servant of God may be thoroughly equipped for every good work." (2 Timothy 3:16–17 - NIV).**

The Word is not just for inspiration—it is for equipping. Every sermon, Bible study, and teaching prepares believers for ministry in their homes, workplaces, and communities. **The church gathers to be trained so it can scatter to serve.**

THE DANGER OF NEGLECTING THE WORD

Amos 8:11 warns:

> **"The days are coming," declares the Sovereign Lord, "when I will send a famine through the land—not a famine of food or a thirst for water, but a famine of hearing the words of the Lord." (NIV).**

We are living in times where many churches are experiencing this famine. Some replace preaching with entertainment. Others dilute the message to avoid offense. But without the pure Word of God, the church starves spiritually.

A healthy church is a Word-centered church. A healthy believer is a Word-filled believer.

PRACTICAL APPLICATION

When you go to church, don't go only to "listen." Go ready to receive and obey. **James 1:22** exhorts us:

> **"Do not merely listen to the word, and so deceive yourselves. Do what it says." (NIV).**

Hearing the Word must lead to action. A sermon that goes in one ear and out the other accomplishes nothing. But when we apply the Word, it bears fruit in our lives (**see Matthew 7:24–25**).

PROPHETIC INSIGHT

God is raising up a church that loves His Word again. The Spirit is restoring a hunger for sound doctrine in a generation drowning in opinions and deception. False teaching may abound, but the true church will stand firm on the unshakable Word of God.

The churches that will endure in these last days will not be built on personalities, preferences, or programs, but on the eternal Word of the Lord, which "stands forever" (**see Isaiah 40:8**).

REFLECTION CHALLENGE

1. Do you approach the Word as a student eager to learn, or as a casual listener?

2. How has the Word preached in church recently convicted, encouraged, or directed you?

3. Are you obeying what you hear, or merely listening without application?

PRAYER OF RENEWAL

"Father, thank You for Your Word that is alive, powerful, and eternal. Forgive me for the times I have taken it lightly or listened without obeying. Give me a hunger for Your truth and a heart that responds in obedience. Let my life be shaped, strengthened, and directed by Your Word. Help me to not only hear but to live out what I receive in church. In Jesus' name. Amen."

STEP OF ACTION

This week, take notes during the sermon at church. Afterward, choose one truth to apply in your life immediately. Share it with a friend or family member, and ask them to hold you accountable to walk it out.

CHAPTER SIX

TO GROW IN FELLOWSHIP AND COMMUNITY

A young believer once said, *"I love Jesus, but I don't need the church."* Over time, however, their faith grew cold, their prayers became rare, and their joy began to fade. Why? Because Christianity was never meant to be lived in isolation. Just as a branch cannot survive without the vine, neither can a Christian thrive without fellowship.

Church is more than a place to worship; it is a family where believers grow together in Christ. God never called us to walk alone. He called us into fellowship, community, and accountability.

GOD'S DESIGN FOR FELLOWSHIP

From the very beginning, God declared, **"It is not good for the man to be alone." (Genesis 2:18 - NIV).** Though this referred to Adam's need for Eve, it reveals a universal truth: we were created for relationship.

The New Testament word for *fellowship* is *koinonia*, which means partnership, sharing, and participation. It is deeper than casual friendship—it is spiritual communion. **Acts 2:42–44** shows us the early church's devotion:

> **"They devoted themselves to the apostles' teaching and to fellowship, to the breaking of bread and to prayer... All the**

**believers were together and had everything in common."
(NIV).**

Fellowship is not optional—it is the lifeblood of the church.

THE "ONE ANOTHER" COMMANDS

The New Testament contains over 50 "one another" commands that
can only be lived out in community. Some examples include:

- **"Love one another." (John 13:34 - NIV).**
- **"Encourage one another." (1 Thessalonians 5:11 - NIV).**
- "Bear one another's burdens." **(see Galatians 6:2)**.
- "Confess your sins to one another and pray for one another."
  (see James 5:16).

These cannot be fulfilled in isolation. To obey Christ fully, we must
be in fellowship with His body.

THE CHURCH AS A SPIRITUAL FAMILY

Paul often described the church in family terms. He called believers
"brothers and sisters" **(see Romans 12:10)** and referred to the
church as "the household of God" **(see Ephesians 2:19)**.

This family is diverse—made up of people from every tribe, tongue,
and nation—yet united in Christ. **Galatians 3:28** declares:

**"There is neither Jew nor Gentile, neither slave nor free,
nor is there male and female, for you are all one in Christ
Jesus." (NIV).**

In the church, social, cultural, and economic barriers are broken down. We become one body, one family, and one community in Christ.

FELLOWSHIP BRINGS STRENGTH

Ecclesiastes 4:9–10 reminds us:

> **"Two are better than one, because they have a good return for their labor: If either of them falls down, one can help the other up. But pity anyone who falls and has no one to help them up." (NIV).**

The Christian walk is filled with trials. Fellowship ensures that we do not face them alone. When one believer is weak, another provides strength. When one is discouraged, another speaks faith. When one falls, another helps them rise.

FELLOWSHIP PROTECTS AGAINST ISOLATION

The enemy's strategy has always been to isolate. A sheep separated from the flock becomes easy prey for wolves. Peter warns us:

> **"Be alert and of sober mind. Your enemy the devil prowls around like a roaring lion looking for someone to devour." (1 Peter 5:8 - NIV).**

Lions hunt by separating one from the herd. In the same way, the enemy attacks isolated believers. Fellowship provides safety and accountability.

PRACTICAL APPLICATION

Fellowship requires intentionality. It is not enough to sit in a pew and leave immediately after the service. True fellowship involves:

- Building relationships.
- Sharing meals.
- Bearing burdens.
- Praying for one another.
- Serving side by side.

When we invest in community, we grow stronger in faith and deeper in love.

PROPHETIC INSIGHT

We live in a culture of independence and isolation. Many prefer online connections to face-to-face fellowship. But the Spirit is restoring authentic community in the church. In these last days, believers will need one another more than ever before. The church will become a true refuge, a place of family, healing, and unity where God's love is revealed to the world.

Jesus declared, **"By this everyone will know that you are my disciples, if you love one another." (John 13:35 - NIV).** The revival the world longs to see will flow through a church marked by love and fellowship.

REFLECTION CHALLENGE

1. Do you see church as a family or just as a weekly service?

2. Are you investing in genuine fellowship, or are you walking in isolation?

3. How can you be more intentional about encouraging, supporting, and loving others in your church community?

PRAYER OF RENEWAL

"Father, thank You for calling me into Your family. Forgive me for any ways I have isolated myself or neglected fellowship. Please help me to build strong, Christ-centered relationships that encourage, strengthen, and sharpen my faith. Make me a source of love and support to my brothers and sisters in Christ. Let my church be a true community where Your love is seen and felt. In Jesus' name. Amen."

STEP OF ACTION

This week, take one step to strengthen fellowship in your church. Invite someone for coffee or a meal, join a small group, or intentionally encourage a brother or sister in Christ. Watch how God uses simple acts of fellowship to grow His body in love.

CHAPTER SEVEN

TO BE EQUIPPED FOR SERVICE

A soldier would never be sent into battle without training, armor, and weapons. To do so would guarantee defeat. In the same way, believers are not meant to go into the spiritual battles of life unequipped. That is why God gave us the church—a training ground where disciples are equipped for service in His kingdom.

Church is not just a place to be comforted; it is a place to be prepared. Every sermon, every act of fellowship, every moment of prayer, and every opportunity to serve is part of God's process of equipping His people for works of ministry.

THE CHURCH AS GOD'S TRAINING GROUND

Paul makes this clear in **Ephesians 4:11–12**:

> **"So Christ Himself gave the apostles, the prophets, the evangelists, the pastors and teachers, to equip his people for works of service, so that the body of Christ may be built up." (NIV).**

Notice: the purpose of leadership in the church is not to do all the work but to equip the saints to do the work of ministry. Church is a spiritual boot camp where believers are trained to live out their calling.

EQUIPPED BY THE WORD

The Word of God is our first tool for equipping. Paul wrote:

> **"All Scripture is God-breathed and is useful for teaching, rebuking, correcting and training in righteousness, so that the servant of God may be thoroughly equipped for every good work." (2 Timothy 3:16–17 - NIV).**

When we hear the Word in church, we are not simply receiving information; we are being trained for transformation and mission. Each message sharpens us, prepares us, and strengthens us to serve effectively.

EQUIPPED BY THE SPIRIT

Beyond teaching, the Holy Spirit equips believers with spiritual gifts. **1 Corinthians 12:7** says:

> **"Now to each one the manifestation of the Spirit is given for the common good." (NIV).**

- Some receive gifts of teaching, prophecy, or encouragement.
- Others receive gifts of healing, helps, or administration.
- All gifts are given not for personal pride, but for building up the body of Christ.

When we gather, these gifts are stirred, developed, and released. A gift unused in isolation finds its purpose in community.

EQUIPPED THROUGH SERVICE

We are not only equipped to serve inside the church but also outside of it. Jesus modeled servant leadership:

> **"For even the Son of Man did not come to be served, but to serve, and to give his life as a ransom for many." (Mark 10:45 - NIV).**

When we gather, we learn how to serve one another, but we are also sent out to serve the world. The church equips us not to sit in pews but to shine in workplaces, schools, neighborhoods, and nations.

THE DANGER OF REMAINING UNEQUIPPED

Hebrews 5:12 warns believers who remain immature:

> **"Though by this time you ought to be teachers, you need someone to teach you the elementary truths of God's word all over again. You need milk, not solid food!" (NIV).**

A believer who refuses to be equipped stays spiritually weak and ineffective. But a believer who submits to the process of equipping grows into maturity, ready to fight the good fight of faith and serve in God's kingdom.

PRACTICAL APPLICATION

Church is not an audience; it is an army. Each time you attend, ask:

- What truth am I being equipped with?
- What gift is God stirring in me?
- How can I use this training to serve others?

The more we embrace equipping, the stronger the body becomes, and the more effective we are in fulfilling the great commission.

PROPHETIC INSIGHT

In these last days, God is mobilizing His church as an army. He is breaking the mindset of spectatorship and raising up equipped, Spirit-filled believers who will take the gospel to the ends of the earth.

The church that equips its members will be a sending church—a lighthouse that not only gathers but also sends disciples into every sphere of society.

REFLECTION CHALLENGE

1. Do you see yourself as part of God's army, equipped for service?

2. Are you actively developing the gifts God has given you through the church?

3. How can you serve both in the church and in your community this week?

PRAYER OF RENEWAL

"Lord, thank You for equipping me through Your Word, Your Spirit, and Your church. Forgive me for any passivity or complacency in my walk. Train me to be a faithful servant and a bold witness. Stir up the gifts within me and show me where to serve in Your body. Make me a vessel prepared for every good work You have ordained. In Jesus' name. Amen."

STEP OF ACTION

This week, identify one area of service in your church and commit to it. Whether greeting, praying, teaching, or helping behind the scenes, take a step to put your training into action.

CHAPTER EIGHT

TO FULFILL THE GREAT COMMISSION

I magine a fire department that never responds to fires. The firefighters meet every week, polish their trucks, and practice drills, but never actually leave the station to rescue anyone. Such a department would fail in its mission.

In the same way, the church does not exist merely to gather but to go. Our purpose is not only worship, fellowship, and growth, but also mission. Every service we attend, every sermon we hear, and every prayer we pray should propel us outward to fulfill Christ's command to make disciples of all nations.

THE GREAT COMMISSION

Before ascending to heaven, Jesus gave His disciples their marching orders:

> **"Therefore go and make disciples of all nations, baptizing them in the name of the Father and of the Son and of the Holy Spirit, and teaching them to obey everything I have commanded you. And surely I am with you always, to the very end of the age." (Matthew 28:19–20 - NIV).**

This is not a suggestion. It is a commission—binding on every believer, every congregation, and every generation.

THE CHURCH AS A MISSION BASE

Acts 1:8 describes the scope of the mission:

> **"But you will receive power when the Holy Spirit comes on you; and you will be my witnesses in Jerusalem, and in all Judea and Samaria, and to the ends of the earth." (NIV).**

Notice the pattern:

- **Jerusalem**—our local community.
- **Judea and Samaria**—the surrounding regions, even to those who are different from us.
- **Ends of the earth**—global missions.

The church equips believers not only to serve one another but also to be witnesses in every sphere of life, both locally and globally.

EVERY BELIEVER IS A WITNESS

Evangelism is not just the job of pastors or missionaries. It is the calling of every believer. **2 Corinthians 5:20** declares:

> **"We are therefore Christ's ambassadors, as though God were making his appeal through us. We implore you on Christ's behalf: Be reconciled to God." (NIV).**

When we leave the church building, we carry the presence of Christ into our homes, workplaces, and communities. We are His ambassadors wherever we go.

DISCIPLESHIP, NOT JUST DECISIONS

The great commission is not merely about making converts; it is about making disciples. Jesus said, **"teaching them to obey everything I have commanded you." (Matthew 28:20 - NIV).**

Church is where discipleship happens—where new believers are taught, nurtured, and equipped to grow into maturity. A church that neglects discipleship is incomplete in its mission.

THE POWER OF THE SPIRIT IN MISSION

The early church fulfilled the great commission through the power of the Holy Spirit. **Acts 17:6** records the testimony of their impact:

> **"These who have turned the world upside down have come here too." (NKJV).**

It wasn't human strength that accomplished this, but Spirit-filled obedience. When the church gathers to pray, worship, and receive the Word, it is empowered to scatter with boldness to witness.

PRACTICAL APPLICATION

Every time we gather for church, we should be asking:

- How is this preparing me to reach the lost?
- How can I share what I've received with someone else?
- Am I living as a witness in my daily life?

Church should never end at the benediction. It continues in the lives we live and the souls we reach throughout the week.

PROPHETIC INSIGHT

In these last days, God is reigniting the fire of evangelism in His church. No longer will services be inward-focused only; they will become launching pads for mission.

The Spirit is calling the church back to urgency—to rescue the lost, to reach the unreached, and to disciple nations. The true measure of a church is not its seating capacity but its sending capacity.

REFLECTION CHALLENGE

1. Do you see the great commission as your personal responsibility or only as the church's responsibility?

2. Are you actively sharing your faith and discipling others, or are you keeping the gospel to yourself?

3. How can your church be more intentional in equipping and sending believers into mission?

PRAYER OF RENEWAL

"Lord Jesus, thank You for entrusting me with Your mission. Forgive me for the times I have stayed silent when I should have spoken, or remained comfortable when I should have gone. Fill me with boldness through Your Spirit to be a faithful witness. Use me in my home, workplace, community, and beyond to share Your love and truth. Let my church be a mission base that impacts the nations. In Jesus' name. Amen."

STEP OF ACTION

This week, pray for one person in your life who does not know Christ. Reach out to them with love—invite them to church, share your testimony, or simply listen to their heart. Take one intentional step toward fulfilling the great commission.

PART III

MISUNDERSTANDINGS AND CHALLENGES

CHAPTER NINE

IT'S NOT ABOUT RELIGION, IT'S ABOUT RELATIONSHIP

A man once attended church every Sunday, sang all the hymns, and gave offerings faithfully. Yet deep inside, he felt empty and unchanged. He had religion, but not relationship. He knew the rituals, but he did not know the Redeemer.

This is the danger many fall into: reducing church to rules, traditions, and routines instead of entering into a living, daily relationship with Jesus Christ. We do not attend church simply to practice religion; we go to encounter the living God, who desires a relationship with His people.

THE DIFFERENCE BETWEEN RELIGION AND RELATIONSHIP

Religion is man's attempt to reach God through rituals and works. Relationship is God reaching down to us through Christ.

- Religion says, *"Do more to earn God's approval."*
- Relationship says, *"It is finished"* (**see John 19:30**).
- Religion produces pride or guilt.
- Relationship produces love and freedom.

Jesus condemned empty religion. In **Matthew 15:8–9**, He said:

"These people honor me with their lips, but their hearts are far from me. They worship me in vain; their teachings are merely human rules." (NIV).

True church attendance is not about outward form, but inward transformation.

JESUS' DESIRE FOR RELATIONSHIP

Jesus did not call His disciples into a religion, but into relationship. In **John 15:15** He told them:

"I no longer call you servants… Instead, I have called you friends, for everything that I learned from my Father I have made known to you." (NIV).

Church is a place where that friendship is nurtured—where we abide in Him, learn from Him, and grow closer to Him.

RELATIONSHIP EXPRESSED IN WORSHIP

When we worship, we are not performing religious rituals; we are drawing near to our Father. **James 4:8** declares:

"Come near to God and he will come near to you." (NIV).

Worship is the language of relationship. It is intimacy with God, not formality before Him.

RELATIONSHIP EXPRESSED IN OBEDIENCE

True relationship leads to obedience. Jesus said in **John 14:15**:

"If you love me, keep my commands." (NIV).

74

Religion obeys out of duty. Relationship obeys out of love. In church, we hear His Word not merely to follow rules, but to please the One we love.

RELATIONSHIP EXPRESSED IN LOVE FOR OTHERS

1 John 4:20 teaches us:

> **"Whoever claims to love God yet hates a brother or sister is a liar. For whoever does not love their brother and sister, whom they have seen, cannot love God, whom they have not seen." (NIV).**

Church is where our relationship with God overflows into relationship with others. If we claim to know Him but do not love His people, our faith is empty.

PRACTICAL APPLICATION

When we go to church, we must ask ourselves:

- Am I here to fulfill a ritual, or to strengthen my relationship with Christ?
- Am I worshiping from the heart, or just going through motions?
- Am I living out my faith in love and obedience?

The church should not be a checklist of religious duties, but a place where our relationship with God deepens.

PROPHETIC INSIGHT

In these last days, God is tearing down forms of empty religion. He is raising up a church of intimacy, not ritual; of passion, not pretense. The Spirit is calling His people back to their first love (**see Revelation 2:4**).

The revival that is coming will not be marked by ritual, but by relationship—people radically in love with Jesus, gathering not out of obligation, but out of a desire for His presence.

REFLECTION CHALLENGE

1. Do you attend church out of routine, or out of hunger for a relationship with God?

2. Is your worship an outward form or an inward expression of love?

3. How does your relationship with Christ show in your love for others?

PRAYER OF RENEWAL

"Father, forgive me for the times I have treated church as a ritual instead of a relationship. Renew in me the joy of intimacy with You. Help me to worship in spirit and in truth, to obey out of love, and to walk closely with You each day. Let my relationship with You overflow into love for Your people. In Jesus' name. Amen."

STEP OF ACTION

This week, set aside intentional time for relational worship. Before Sunday service, spend 15 minutes alone with God in prayer, not asking for anything, but simply thanking Him and drawing near in love. Bring that posture into church and notice the difference in your worship.

CHAPTER TEN

WHEN CHURCH BECOMES ABOUT US INSTEAD OF GOD

A visitor once attended a church where the lights were dazzling, the music professional, and the programs well-organized. Yet, after leaving, he said, *"I saw everything but God."*

This is the danger when church becomes centered on us—our preferences, our comfort, our entertainment—rather than on God. A church built around people's desires instead of God's presence may draw crowds, but it will lack power.

THE DANGER OF SELF-CENTERED WORSHIP

True worship is God-centered. **Psalm 115:1** reminds us:

> **"Not to us, O Lord, not to us but to Your name be the glory, because of Your love and faithfulness." (NIV).**

But when church becomes about us, we start asking the wrong questions:

- *"Did I like the worship?"* instead of *"Did God receive my worship?"*

- *"Was the sermon entertaining?"* instead of *"Did the Word convict and transform me?"*

- *"Did I feel comfortable?"* instead of *"Was Christ exalted?"*

Self-centered worship reduces God to a performer and the congregation to an audience. But true worship makes God the focus, and the church His participants.

THE EXAMPLE OF ISRAEL

In the Old Testament, Israel often drifted into self-centered worship. In **Isaiah 29:13**, God said:

> **"These people come near to me with their mouth and honor me with their lips, but their hearts are far from me. Their worship of me is based on merely human rules they have been taught." (NIV).**

Though they offered sacrifices, their hearts were not surrendered. In the same way, modern churches may have activity, programs, and noise—yet still miss God if their hearts are not focused on Him.

JESUS CLEANSING THE TEMPLE

Jesus confronted this problem head-on when He cleansed the temple. In **Matthew 21:13** He declared:

> **"It is written," he said to them, "'My house will be called a house of prayer,' but you are making it 'a den of robbers.'" (NIV).**

The temple had become a marketplace centered on human gain rather than God's glory. Likewise, if we are not careful, our churches can become platforms for performance, popularity, or profit instead of altars of worship.

CHURCH IS ABOUT GOD'S GLORY

The primary purpose of church is to glorify God. **Ephesians 3:21** declares:

> **"To Him be glory in the church and in Christ Jesus throughout all generations, forever and ever! Amen." (NIV).**

Every song sung, every sermon preached, every prayer lifted should magnify Christ. When God's glory is the focus, His presence fills the house, His people are transformed, and the lost are drawn to Him.

PRACTICAL APPLICATION

We must examine our hearts when we go to church:

- Am I coming to be entertained, or to encounter God?
- Do I expect the church to cater to me, or do I come to offer myself as a living sacrifice (**see Romans 12:1**)?
- Do I measure the service by how much I received, or by how much God was glorified?

Church must shift from being about consumerism to being about Christ-centeredness.

PROPHETIC INSIGHT

The Spirit of God is purifying His church in this hour. The churches built on entertainment will fade, but the churches built on prayer, worship, and God's glory will endure. A new move of God is coming that will strip away distractions, pride, and performance, leaving only the raw presence of Jesus.

The Lord is asking His church: *"Will you make room for Me again? Will you return to My presence and My glory?"*

REFLECTION CHALLENGE

1. Do you approach church with a "consumer" mindset, or with a heart of worship and surrender?

2. How can you shift your focus from what you get out of church to what you give to God in church?

3. Is your church centered on God's glory, or have we allowed human preferences and entertainment to take over?

PRAYER OF RENEWAL

"Lord, forgive me for the times I have made church about myself instead of You. Cleanse my heart of selfishness and distraction. Restore in me a spirit of true worship that exalts You alone. Let my church be a house where Your presence dwells, Your Word is honored, and Your glory is revealed. In Jesus' name. Amen."

STEP OF ACTION

This week, go to church with a different question in your heart: not *"What will I get today?"* but *"What can I give to God today?"* Offer Him your full worship, your attention to His Word, and your willingness to serve.

CHAPTER ELEVEN

OVERCOMING EXCUSES FOR NOT GOING

One of the most common struggles believers face today is not a lack of opportunity to worship but a list of excuses for why they can't or won't attend church. Excuses are easy to create, but they rob us of blessings, weaken our spiritual growth, and often expose misplaced priorities.

THE DANGER OF EXCUSES

Jesus Himself addressed this issue in the parable of the great banquet. In **Luke 14:18–20**, we read:

> **"But they all alike began to make excuses. The first said, 'I have just bought a field, and I must go and see it. Please excuse me.' Another said, 'I have just bought five yoke of oxen, and I'm on my way to try them out. Please excuse me.' Still another said, 'I just got married, so I can't come.'" (NIV).**

Each excuse seemed valid in the natural, but in the spiritual, it revealed misplaced priorities. Their blessings (property, business, marriage) became the very distractions that kept them from God's invitation.

MODERN-DAY EXCUSES

Today, we hear similar excuses:

- *"I'm too tired."*
- *"I can watch online later."*
- *"The church is full of hypocrites."*
- *"I don't feel like going."*
- *"Sunday is my only free day to rest."*

Although these may seem real, they are ultimately obstacles that prevent us from obeying God's command not to forsake the assembly (**see Hebrews 10:25**).

WHY EXCUSES DON'T STAND BEFORE GOD

1. Excuses reveal misplaced priorities. When something is truly important, we make time for it. Jesus said in **Matthew 6:33**: **"But seek first his kingdom and his righteousness, and all these things will be given to you as well." (NIV).**

2. Excuses rob us of fellowship and growth. **Proverbs 27:17** says: **"As iron sharpens iron, so one person sharpens another." (NIV).** Staying home keeps us from the sharpening that comes only through community.

3. Excuses give the enemy room to isolate us. **1 Peter 5:8** warns: **"Be alert and of sober mind. Your enemy the devil prowls around like a roaring lion looking for someone to devour." (NIV).** Sheep that wander from the flock are easy prey for wolves.

THE CALL TO COMMITMENT

God is not calling us to convenience but to commitment. **Romans 12:1** urges us:

> **"Therefore, I urge you, brothers and sisters, in view of God's mercy, to offer your bodies as a living sacrifice, holy and pleasing to God—this is your true and proper worship." (NIV).**

This means showing up, even when it's not easy, because our worship is not based on feelings but on faithfulness.

BIBLICAL EXAMPLES OF DETERMINED WORSHIP

- Hannah (**see 1 Samuel 1:9–19**): Despite her pain and ridicule, she went to the house of God and poured out her soul.

- The Early Church (**see Acts 2:42–47**): They devoted themselves daily to the apostles' teaching, fellowship, breaking of bread, and prayer.

- The Shunammite Woman (**see 2 Kings 4:22–23**): When her son died, she still made her way to the man of God, declaring, *"It is well."*

These examples remind us that excuses lose power when faith takes priority.

PRACTICAL WAYS TO OVERCOME EXCUSES

1. **Plan ahead.** Treat church as a non-negotiable appointment.

2. **Prepare your heart and home.** Set clothes, Bibles, and schedules in order the night before.

3. **Partner with accountability.** Go with family, friends, or a prayer partner who will encourage you when you feel weak.

4. **Pray for renewed desire.** Ask God to give you joy and hunger for His house (**see Psalm 122:1**).

PROPHETIC INSIGHT

The Lord is raising up a remnant of believers who will not be swayed by excuses, distractions, or cultural apathy. These are the ones who will keep the fire of God burning in their churches and their families. The Spirit is asking in this hour: *"Will you lay aside excuses and return to My house with passion?"*

REFLECTION CHALLENGE

- What excuse have you used most often for missing church?

- Does your schedule reveal that God is truly first in your life?

- What steps can you take this week to prioritize God's house above convenience?

PRAYER OF COMMITMENT

"Father, forgive me for the times I have allowed excuses to keep me from Your house. Remove the spirit of complacency and renew in me a hunger for Your presence and Your Word. Strengthen my faith, align my priorities, and let me be found faithful in Your house. In Jesus' name. Amen."

STEP OF ACTION

This week, identify one excuse you've used for skipping church and replace it with a faith-filled action. If tiredness is the excuse, go to bed earlier on Saturday. If convenience is the excuse, remind yourself: *"I go not for convenience, but for Christ."*

PART IV

THE BLESSING OF BELONGING

CHAPTER TWELVE

THE BLESSING OF CONSISTENCY IN ATTENDANCE

One of the greatest secrets of spiritual growth is not found in occasional spiritual highs but in consistent devotion. Just as a healthy body requires regular nourishment, a strong spirit requires consistent fellowship in God's house. Inconsistency weakens us, but consistency produces strength, stability, and blessing.

THE POWER OF CONSISTENCY

The Bible repeatedly points to the blessings that come from steadfastness.

- **Psalm 92:13–14: "Those who are planted in the house of the Lord shall flourish in the courts of our God. They shall still bear fruit in old age; they shall be fresh and flourishing." (NKJV).**

Flourishing is not promised to those who occasionally visit but to those who are planted.

- **1 Corinthians 15:58: "Therefore, my beloved brothers, be steadfast, immovable, always abounding in the work of the Lord, knowing that in the Lord your labor is not in vain." (NKJV).**

Stability in the Lord leads to abounding fruit.

CONSISTENCY PRODUCES SPIRITUAL GROWTH

When believers attend church faithfully, they:

1. **Grow in the Word.** Faith comes by hearing (**see Romans 10:17**), and consistent hearing builds a strong foundation.

2. **Strengthen relationships.** Fellowship deepens when believers gather regularly, not occasionally.

3. **Develop discipline.** Regular worship builds habits that protect us when trials come.

4. **Leave a legacy.** Families who model consistency pass faith to the next generation (**see Deuteronomy 6:6–7**).

INCONSISTENCY WEAKENS FAITH

Hebrews 10:25 warns us:

> **"Not forsaking the assembling of ourselves together, as is the manner of some, but exhorting one another—and so much the more as you see the Day approaching." (NKJV).**

Those who drift in and out of church often drift in and out of spiritual strength. Spiritual inconsistency breeds spiritual vulnerability.

BIBLICAL EXAMPLES OF CONSISTENT WORSHIP

- **Daniel (see Daniel 6:10):** He prayed three times a day, even when threatened with death.

- **The Early Church (see Acts 2:46–47):** They met daily with gladness and sincerity of heart, and the Lord added to their number.

- **Jesus Himself (see Luke 4:16):** It was His custom to go into the synagogue on the Sabbath.

If consistency marked Jesus and the apostles, it must also mark us.

PRACTICAL BENEFITS OF CONSISTENCY IN CHURCH ATTENDANCE

1. **Peace in storms.** Regular exposure to God's Word equips us to face trials.

2. **Direction in life.** Sermons, prayers, and counsel give clarity in decision-making.

3. **Covering and accountability.** A consistent believer is less likely to wander from the faith unnoticed.

4. **Anointing overflow.** The more we show up, the more we position ourselves under the outpouring of God's Spirit.

THE BLESSING ON FAMILIES

Joshua declared in **Joshua 24:15**:

**"...as for me and my house, we will serve the Lord."
(NKJV).**

Families that consistently gather in God's house raise children who know the value of worship. Consistency becomes an inheritance passed down through generations.

REFLECTION CHALLENGE

- Are you consistent in attending church, or do you allow distractions and excuses to break your pattern?

- Do your family and friends see your faithfulness as an example to follow?

- How might your spiritual life change if you committed to greater consistency in gathering with believers?

PRAYER FOR FAITHFULNESS

"Lord, thank You for the blessing that comes through consistency. Help me to be steadfast, unshaken by excuses, and firmly planted in Your house. Let my faithfulness bear fruit in my life, my family, and my church. May I be found faithful until the day You call me home. In Jesus' name. Amen."

STEP OF ACTION

This week, create a practical plan: set a consistent time for worship, both in your church gatherings and in your personal devotions. Refuse to let inconsistency rob you of the blessings of being planted.

CHAPTER THIRTEEN

CHURCH AS A PLACE OF HEALING

L ife is filled with pain, brokenness, and wounds—both visible and invisible. Many walk through church doors not because they are whole but because they are hurting. The church is not a museum for the perfect; it is a hospital for the broken. In God's house, healing flows through His Word, His Spirit, and His people.

THE CHURCH AS GOD'S HEALING STATION

Jesus declared in **Luke 4:18**:

> **"The Spirit of the Lord is upon me, because He has anointed me to preach the gospel to the poor; He has sent me to heal the brokenhearted, to proclaim liberty to the captives and recovery of sight to the blind, to set at liberty those who are oppressed." (NKJV).**

The mission of Christ is still the mission of His church. Every gathering should be a place where the brokenhearted are restored and those bound are set free.

- **Psalm 147:3: "He heals the brokenhearted and binds up their wounds." (NKJV).**

- **Matthew 11:28: "Come to Me, all you who labor and are heavy laden, and I will give you rest." (NKJV).**

HEALING IN WORSHIP

There is a mysterious and beautiful healing that comes when God's people worship together.

- **2 Corinthians 3:17: "Now the Lord is the Spirit; and where the Spirit of the Lord is, there is liberty." (NKJV).**

- During heartfelt worship, chains of fear, shame, and grief often fall away.

- Praise becomes a spiritual medicine, lifting burdens and restoring joy (**see Isaiah 61:3**).

HEALING THROUGH THE WORD

God's Word has the power to mend what doctors and counselors cannot.

- **Proverbs 4:20–22: "My son, give attention to my words... For they are life to those who find them, and health to all their flesh." (NKJV).**

- Every sermon preached carries potential for healing—whether in spirit, soul, or body.

HEALING THROUGH FELLOWSHIP

God often uses the people in the church as instruments of healing.

- **James 5:16: "Confess your trespasses to one another, and pray for one another, that you may be healed. The effective, fervent prayer of a righteous man avails much." (NKJV).**

- Community care—praying, encouraging, listening—becomes a channel of God's restoring grace.

The church family embraces the wounded and reminds them they are not alone.

THE EXAMPLE OF THE EARLY CHURCH

In Acts 3, Peter and John encountered a lame man at the temple gate. He received not only physical healing but also spiritual restoration as he walked into the temple, leaping and praising God.

The same God still heals today in His house. The church must continue to be a place where miracles are expected and testimonies abound.

PRACTICAL WAYS THE CHURCH BRINGS HEALING

1. Through preaching that brings conviction and hope.

2. Through prayer teams and altar calls, where burdens are lifted.

3. Through counseling and discipleship that guide believers into wholeness.

4. Through love and acceptance that break the spirit of rejection.

REFLECTION CHALLENGE

- Have you allowed the church to be a place of healing, or have you carried your wounds in silence?

- How can you help your local church be a hospital for the hurting?

- Are you willing to be an instrument of God's healing to someone else in the body of Christ?

PRAYER FOR HEALING

"Lord, I thank You that Your church is a place of restoration. Heal every hidden wound, mend every broken heart, and bring wholeness where there has been pain. Use me as a vessel of encouragement and compassion to others who are hurting. Let Your house always be a sanctuary of healing, hope, and restoration. In Jesus' name. Amen."

STEP OF ACTION

This week, identify one person in your church who is hurting and offer to pray with them, visit them, or simply listen. As you extend healing, you will also receive healing.

CHAPTER FOURTEEN

THE CHURCH AND COMMUNITY IMPACT

The church is not called to exist in isolation. Its presence must make a visible, tangible difference in the community around it. A church that only blesses those inside its walls is incomplete. Jesus declared in **Matthew 5:14**:

> **"You are the light of the world. A city that is set on a hill cannot be hidden." (NKJV).**

When the church shines its light, entire neighborhoods, cities, and nations are transformed.

THE CHURCH AS SALT AND LIGHT

- **Matthew 5:13: "You are the salt of the earth; but if the salt loses its flavor, how shall it be seasoned?" (NKJV).**

- The church preserves morality in society and prevents the decay of sin.

- **Matthew 5:14–16** calls the church to be visible, not hidden, and to do good works that glorify God.

The impact of a healthy church cannot be measured solely by numbers—it is evident in transformed lives, restored families, and healed communities.

THE EARLY CHURCH'S COMMUNITY IMPACT

- **Acts 2:44–47** shows the believers sharing with those in need, breaking bread together, and winning the favor of all people.

- Their unity and generosity were a powerful testimony that drew others to Christ daily.

A true New Testament church doesn't just gather—it gives. It feeds the hungry, clothes the naked, and lifts the oppressed.

THE CHURCH AS AN ADVOCATE FOR JUSTICE AND MERCY

- **Micah 6:8: "He has shown you, O man, what is good; and what does the Lord require of you but to do justly, to love mercy, and to walk humbly with your God?" (NKJV).**

- The church must raise its voice against injustice, defend the vulnerable, and extend mercy to the broken.

When the church actively stands for righteousness, communities begin to reflect the heart of God.

PRACTICAL WAYS THE CHURCH IMPACTS COMMUNITIES

1. **Through outreach programs** – food drives, clothing banks, shelters, and community support.

2. **Through education** – Bible schools, tutoring, and mentoring programs for youth.

3. **Through healthcare support** – prayer, counseling, and sometimes medical missions.

4. **Through advocacy** – speaking up for those who cannot speak for themselves (**see Proverbs 31:8–9**).

5. **Through love in action** – intentional kindness that opens doors for the gospel.

SCRIPTURES ON COMMUNITY IMPACT

- **Jeremiah 29:7: "And seek the peace of the city where I have caused you to be carried away captive, and pray to the Lord for it; for in its peace you will have peace." (NKJV).**

- **James 1:27: "Pure and undefiled religion before God and the Father is this: to visit orphans and widows in their trouble, and to keep oneself unspotted from the world." (NKJV).**

- **Galatians 6:10: "Therefore, as we have opportunity, let us do good to all, especially to those who are of the household of faith." (NKJV).**

REFLECTION CHALLENGE

- Does your church's presence make your community better?

- Are you personally involved in being salt and light beyond the church walls?

- What one step can you take this week to extend God's love into your neighborhood?

PRAYER FOR COMMUNITY IMPACT

"Father, thank You for planting Your church as a beacon of light in every community. Please help me see the needs around me and be part of the solution. Let my life and my church reflect Your justice, Your mercy, and Your love to a hurting world. Make us a city on a hill that cannot be hidden. In Jesus' name. Amen."

STEP OF ACTION

This week, look for one practical way to serve your community. It may be volunteering, giving, or simply showing kindness to someone overlooked. Write it down, commit to it, and do it as unto the Lord.

PART V

THE CALL TO COMMITMENT

CHAPTER FIFTEEN

THE FUTURE OF THE CHURCH

The church has always faced trials, persecutions, and shifting cultures, yet Jesus' promise stands sure: **Matthew 16:18 – "I will build My church, and the gates of Hades shall not prevail against it." (NKJV).**

The future of the church is not in the hands of governments, culture, or even human opinion—it is in the hands of Christ, the eternal Head of the church. Though the world grows darker, the church will shine brighter until the day He returns.

THE CHURCH WILL ENDURE

- **Isaiah 9:7: "Of the increase of His government and peace there will be no end." (NKJV).**

- The church is not shrinking—it is expanding, even in places where it seems silenced. Underground churches in persecuted nations testify that nothing can stop the spread of the gospel.

While earthly kingdoms rise and fall, the church remains unshaken because it is built upon Christ the Solid Rock.

THE CHURCH AND END-TIME PROPHECY

- **Matthew 24:14: "And this gospel of the kingdom will be preached in all the world as a witness to all the nations, and then the end will come." (NKJV).**

- The future of the church is deeply tied to the great commission. Before Christ's return, the church will play the central role of proclaiming the gospel to every tribe, tongue, and nation.

The church is not waiting to escape the world—it is called to fulfill its mission until the trumpet sounds.

THE CHURCH WILL FACE OPPOSITION

- **2 Timothy 3:1 warns: "But know this, that in the last days perilous times will come." (NKJV).**

- Yet even in hardship, the church thrives. Persecution has never extinguished the flame of faith—it has only caused it to burn brighter.

Every challenge to the church is an opportunity for the Spirit of God to demonstrate His power and preserve His people.

THE CHURCH'S GLORIOUS DESTINY

- **Ephesians 5:27 declares that Christ will present to Himself "a glorious church, not having spot or wrinkle or any such thing, but that she should be holy and without blemish." (NKJV).**

- The church is moving toward glory. Every trial, every season of pruning, is preparing her for her Bridegroom.

The final chapter of the church is not defeat, but victory. The people of God will reign with Christ forever.

SCRIPTURES ON THE FUTURE OF THE CHURCH

- **Daniel 2:44: "And in the days of these kings the God of heaven will set up a kingdom which shall never be destroyed." (NKJV).**

- **Revelation 21:2–3: "Then I, John, saw the holy city, New Jerusalem, coming down out of heaven from God, prepared as a bride adorned for her husband." (NKJV).**

- **Hebrews 12:28: "Therefore, since we are receiving a kingdom which cannot be shaken, let us have grace, by which we may serve God acceptably with reverence and godly fear." (NKJV).**

REFLECTION CHALLENGE

- Are you living with urgency, knowing the church has an eternal mission?

- Do you see yourself as part of Christ's victorious church, or do you allow fear and culture to dictate your outlook?

- Are you helping prepare the church for her Bridegroom, or are you distracted by the temporary things of this world?

PRAYER FOR THE FUTURE OF THE CHURCH

"Lord Jesus, thank You that You are building Your church and that nothing can stop it. Help me to live faithfully, with my eyes fixed on the eternal future You have promised. Keep me steadfast, unmovable, and always abounding in Your work. Prepare me, along with Your church, to be a spotless bride awaiting Your return. In Jesus' name. Amen."

STEP OF ACTION

This week, take time to pray for the global church—those in persecuted nations, those on the mission field, and those struggling with compromise. Ask God to strengthen His people and to help you remain faithful to His mission until the end.

CHAPTER 16

BECOMING THE CHURCH, NOT JUST ATTENDING

For many, church is viewed as a place—a building with walls, pews, stained glass, and pulpits. But biblically, church is not a building; it is a body of people redeemed by the blood of Christ and empowered by the Holy Spirit. Jesus declared, **"For where two or three are gathered together in My name, I am there in the midst of them." (Matthew 18:20 - NKJV).** The presence of God is not confined to an address on a street corner—it dwells in the hearts of His people.

Too often, believers stop at attending church rather than being the church. Attending church is valuable—we are commanded not to forsake assembling together (**see Hebrews 10:25**). But attendance without transformation and mission reduces the Christian walk to a ritual. Becoming the church means embracing our calling to be living witnesses and carriers of God's presence wherever we go.

LIVING AS WITNESSES DAILY

Jesus never said, *"Go to church and keep it within four walls."* Instead, He commissioned us: **"Go into all the world and preach the gospel to all creation." (Mark 16:15 - NKJV).** The early church understood this truth. Their meetings were powerful, but their witness outside the gathering shook cities, shifted cultures, and advanced the kingdom.

111

- The church at Antioch (**see Acts 11:19–26**) didn't just gather; they evangelized, discipled, and sent missionaries.

- The church in **Acts 8** scattered due to persecution, yet they carried the gospel with them wherever they went.

A true believer is not only a Sunday worshipper but a Monday witness. We are called to live Christ-centered lives in our homes, workplaces, schools, and communities. Jesus told His disciples, **"But you shall receive power when the Holy Spirit has come upon you; and you shall be witnesses to Me in Jerusalem, and in all Judea and Samaria, and to the end of the earth." (Acts 1:8 - NKJV).** Witnessing is not optional; it is identity.

Daily witnessing doesn't always mean preaching sermons. Sometimes it is:

- Living with integrity at work.
- Showing kindness where others show cruelty.
- Sharing Christ in conversations naturally, not forcefully.
- Praying for those in need.

As Paul wrote, **"Now then, we are ambassadors for Christ, as though God were pleading through us: we implore you on Christ's behalf, be reconciled to God." (2 Corinthians 5:20 - NKJV).** To become the church is to accept our role as ambassadors every single day.

CARRYING THE PRESENCE OF GOD EVERYWHERE

When Israel carried the Ark of the Covenant, they carried the visible symbol of God's presence. But now, through Christ and the indwelling of the Holy Spirit, we are the temples of the living God. Paul reminds us: **"Or do you not know that your body is the temple of the Holy Spirit who is in you, whom you have from God, and you are not your own?" (1 Corinthians 6:19 - NKJV).**

This changes everything. The presence of God is not locked in the sanctuary—it goes with us into grocery stores, boardrooms, classrooms, and neighborhoods. Wherever believers go, the atmosphere should shift because the presence of God is carried within them.

- Joseph carried God's presence into Egypt, turning slavery and prison into platforms for God's glory (**see Genesis 39:2–3**).

- Daniel carried God's presence into Babylon, where kings recognized the Spirit of the Holy God in him (**see Daniel 5:14**).

- The apostles carried God's presence so powerfully that Peter's shadow brought healing (**see Acts 5:15**).

We must ask: When I walk into a room, does the presence of God go with me? Do people sense Christ in my speech, attitude, and conduct?

Becoming the church means that we don't wait for Sunday to experience God's presence—we walk daily as bearers of His glory.

PRACTICAL APPLICATION

1. **Shift your mindset:** Church is not just a weekly event—it is your identity.

2. **Be intentional daily:** Look for opportunities to be a witness—through acts of kindness, words of encouragement, and sharing Christ's love.

3. **Guard His presence:** Stay prayed up, worship often, and live holy so His Spirit flows freely through you.

4. **Engage culture with kingdom values:** Shine the light of Christ in dark places. As Jesus said, **"You are the light of the world. A town built on a hill cannot be hidden" (Matthew 5:14).**

REFLECTION QUESTIONS

1. Do you view church primarily as a building you attend or a body you belong to?

2. How are you living as a daily witness in your workplace, home, or community?

3. In what ways can you better carry the presence of God into every environment you enter?

DECLARATION

"I am not just a churchgoer—I am the church. I will live as a witness daily, carrying the presence of God into every place I step. I am

Christ's ambassador, His temple, and His light in the world. Through me, others will encounter Jesus."

PRAYER

Heavenly Father, thank You for reminding me that I am not just called to attend church, but to be the church. Help me to live as Your witness daily, in word and in action. Teach me to carry Your presence everywhere I go, so that my life becomes a reflection of Your love, power, and truth. May I be an instrument through which many come to know You. In Jesus' name. Amen.

CHAPTER 17

THE CHURCH OF THE FUTURE: PREPARING THE BRIDE OF CHRIST

The church of Jesus Christ is not merely an institution in time—it is an eternal body with a divine destiny. While the world sees the church as an earthly organization, scripture reveals it as the bride of Christ, chosen, redeemed, and being prepared for a glorious union with her Bridegroom. The church is moving toward its ultimate future: standing before Christ, clothed in righteousness, spotless and blameless, ready for the great marriage supper of the Lamb.

Paul wrote with great clarity: **"Husbands, love your wives, just as Christ also loved the church and gave Himself for her, that He might sanctify and cleanse her with the washing of water by the word, that He might present her to Himself a glorious church, not having spot or wrinkle or any such thing, but that she should be holy and without blemish." (Ephesians 5:25–27 - NKJV).** This is the picture of the church of the future—the glorious bride prepared for eternity.

THE GLORIOUS CHURCH WITHOUT SPOT OR WRINKLE

The church has walked through centuries of trials—persecution, compromise, revival, reformation, and restoration. Yet, Christ is still sanctifying His bride. Just as Esther was prepared with oils and perfumes before being presented to the king (**see Esther 2:12**), the church is undergoing purification by the Spirit and the Word in preparation for her eternal moment.

1. **A Purified Church** – Christ will not return for a lukewarm or divided church, but one made holy by His Spirit. **"And everyone who has this hope in Him purifies himself, just as He is pure" (1 John 3:3 - NKJV).**

2. **A Radiant Church** – Not hidden in shame, but shining in the beauty of holiness. **"Arise, shine, for your light has come! And the glory of the Lord rises upon you" (Isaiah 60:1 - NKJV).**

3. **A Victorious Church** – The gates of hell will not prevail against it (**see Matthew 16:18**). Despite earthly opposition, the church will triumph because its foundation is Christ Himself.

Just as a bride prepares herself with care and devotion for her wedding day, the church must live with urgency, expectancy, and holiness in preparation for the coming of the Lord.

THE ETERNAL GATHERING IN HEAVEN

The church of the future is not confined to time. It is destined for eternity, where believers from every nation, tribe, and language will gather before the throne. John saw this vision: **"After these things I looked, and behold, a great multitude which no one could number, of all nations, tribes, peoples, and tongues, standing**

before the throne and before the Lamb" (Revelation 7:9 - NKJV).

The marriage supper of the Lamb is the culmination of the church's journey. **Revelation 19:7–8** declares: **"Let us rejoice and be glad and give him glory! For the wedding of the Lamb has come, and his bride has made herself ready. Fine linen, bright and clean, was given her to wear." (NIV).**

This eternal gathering will be the ultimate celebration:

- No more division between denominations.

- No more tears, pain, or persecution.

- Every saint, from the apostles to the martyrs to present-day believers, will worship the Lamb together.

The church's destiny is not merely survival in a broken world but glorification in the eternal presence of Christ.

PREPARING AS THE BRIDE

If this is the future of the church, how should we live now? Preparation is not passive—it requires active faithfulness.

- **Holiness** – Living in purity, resisting compromise, and walking in righteousness **(see 2 Corinthians 7:1)**.

- **Intimacy** – Cultivating deep fellowship with Christ through prayer, worship, and obedience **(see John 15:4–5)**.

- **Readiness** – Watching and waiting for His return, like the wise virgins who kept their lamps burning (**see Matthew 25:1–13**).

- **Unity** – Striving for oneness in the body of Christ, because the Bride must be united when presented to her Groom (**see John 17:21**).

We are not preparing for an event—we are preparing for a Person. The Bridegroom is coming, and the bride must be ready.

PRACTICAL APPLICATION

1. Examine your life and ask: *Am I living in a way that honors Christ's coming?*

2. Commit daily to holiness and intimacy with God.

3. See the church not as a building or program but as an eternal family.

4. Keep your hope fixed on eternity, not temporary things.

REFLECTION QUESTIONS

1. Do you see yourself as part of the Bride of Christ, preparing for His return?

2. Are you allowing the Word of God to wash and purify you daily?

3. What distractions or compromises do you need to lay aside to prepare for the eternal gathering?

DECLARATION

"I am part of the Bride of Christ. I am being washed, purified, and prepared for His coming. I will live holy, walk in love, and carry the hope of eternity in my heart. I belong to the victorious, radiant, and eternal church of the living God."

CLOSING PRAYER

Lord Jesus, thank You for loving Your church so deeply that You gave Yourself for her. I long to be part of that glorious bride, without spot or wrinkle, ready for Your coming. Wash me daily with Your Word, purify my heart, and help me to walk in holiness and devotion. May my life reflect the beauty of a bride preparing for her Bridegroom. Keep my eyes fixed on eternity, and may I never lose sight of the hope of the marriage supper of the Lamb. In Your precious name. Amen.

CONCLUSION

RETURNING TO THE HEART OF THE CHURCH

A JOURNEY COMPLETED, A CALL RENEWED

We began this journey with a simple but profound question: *Why do we go to church?* Along the way, we discovered that the answer is not found in habit, tradition, or social obligation, but in the very heart of God's design for His people.

The church is more than a building, a service, or a weekly event—it is the living body of Christ. It is the family of God, the training ground of disciples, the place where burdens are lifted, and the house where God's presence dwells.

As we close these chapters, the call to every reader is clear: Do not forsake the assembling of yourselves together (**see Hebrews 10:25**). Do not reduce church to something casual, optional, or secondary. Instead, see it as a divine priority—God's way of shaping His people for eternity.

THE ETERNAL VALUE OF THE CHURCH

The church is the only institution Jesus promised to build Himself. He did not say He would build governments, corporations, or movements—but He declared:

Matthew 16:18 – "And I tell you that you are Peter, and on this rock I will build my church, and the gates of Hades will not overcome it." (NIV).

The church has eternal value because it is God's chosen vessel to proclaim His gospel, disciple His people, and reveal His kingdom on earth.

When you invest in the church, you are investing in eternity. When you serve the church, you are serving Christ Himself. When you remain faithful to the fellowship, you are positioning yourself for spiritual growth, protection, and purpose.

A WARNING AGAINST NEGLECT

To walk away from the church is to walk away from God's ordained covering. Many have drifted due to offense, disappointment, or complacency, but the consequence of spiritual isolation is weakness, vulnerability, and a loss of direction.

The enemy knows that a disconnected believer is a powerless believer. That is why scripture continually calls us to unity, to gathering, and to faithfulness in fellowship.

Ecclesiastes 4:9–10 – "Two are better than one, because they have a good reward for their labor. For if they fall, one will lift up his companion. But woe to him who is alone when he falls, for he has no one to help him up." (NIV).

A CALL TO COMMITMENT

As you finish this book, I urge you to make a personal commitment: **I will not just go to church—I will be the church.**

- Be present, not absent.
- Be engaged, not distracted.
- Be a participant, not just a spectator.
- Be a servant, not just a consumer.

The church thrives when its people rise. Your presence matters. Your prayers matter. Your gifts matter. Your service matters.

SCRIPTURES FOR THE JOURNEY AHEAD

- **Psalm 92:13 – "Those who are planted in the house of the Lord shall flourish in the courts of our God." (NKJV).**

- **Acts 2:42 – "And they continued steadfastly in the apostles' doctrine and fellowship, in the breaking of bread, and in prayers." (NKJV).**

- **Ephesians 4:16 – "From whom the whole body, joined and knit together by what every joint supplies, according to the effective working by which every part does its share, causes growth of the body for the edifying of itself in love." (NKJV).**

REFLECTION CHALLENGE

- Are you faithfully planted in the house of God, or are you drifting?

- Do you view church as optional or essential?

- How can you better serve, give, and participate in the life of your local church?

- What legacy will you leave behind in the church for the next generation?

A CLOSING PRAYER

"Father, thank You for the gift of Your church—the body of Christ, the family of faith, the house of Your presence. Forgive me for the times I have neglected or undervalued it. Today, I renew my commitment to be faithful, steadfast, and planted in Your house. Use me for Your glory, and let my life be a testimony of the power of Your church in the world. In Jesus' name. Amen."

FINAL STEP OF ACTION

Do not let this book end on paper—let it continue in your life. Commit today:

- Be consistent in attending church.
- Seek ways to serve in your local congregation.
- Encourage others to return to the house of God.
- Pray for the future of the church daily.

The church is not perfect, but it is God's chosen instrument. And when Christ returns, He will return not for individuals in isolation, but for a glorious bride prepared and waiting. May you be found among the faithful, ready, and rooted in His house.

www.ingramcontent.com/pod-product-compliance
Lightning Source LLC
LaVergne TN
LVHW021520080426
835509LV00018B/2565